Table Of Contents

Introduction

The popularity of mobile gaming

The popularity of mobile gaming has been on the rise in recent years, and it shows no signs of slowing down. With the widespread availability of smartphones and tablets, mobile gaming has become a convenient and accessible form of entertainment for people of all ages.

One of the main reasons for the popularity of mobile gaming is its convenience. Players can access their favorite games anytime, anywhere, without the need for a dedicated gaming console or PC. This makes mobile gaming an ideal option for people who are always on the go and want to enjoy a quick gaming session during their commute or lunch break.

Another reason for the popularity of mobile gaming is the sheer variety of games available. From casual puzzle games to action-packed shooters and MMOs, there is a mobile game for everyone. Whether you prefer single-player experiences or multiplayer battles, there is no shortage of options to choose from.

Mobile gaming is also an affordable option compared to traditional gaming. Most mobile games are free to download and play, with optional in-app purchases for additional content or features. This makes mobile gaming an ideal choice for people who want to enjoy gaming without breaking the bank.

The social aspect of mobile gaming is another reason for its popularity. Many mobile games allow players to connect and play with friends or other players from around the world. This creates a sense of community and camaraderie among gamers, which can enhance the overall gaming experience.

In conclusion, the popularity of mobile gaming is a testament to the convenience, variety, affordability, and social aspects of this form of entertainment. As mobile technology continues to evolve, we can expect to see even more innovative and exciting mobile games in the future.

Whether you are a casual gamer or a hardcore enthusiast, there has never been a better time to dive into the world of mobile gaming.

The importance of choosing the right game engine

When it comes to developing a mobile game, choosing the right game engine is crucial. The game engine is the software that provides the necessary tools to create a game, including graphics, physics, sound, and more. In this subchapter, we'll explore the importance of choosing the right game engine and how it can impact the success of your mobile game.

First and foremost, the game engine you choose will determine the capabilities of your game. Some game engines are better suited for certain types of games, such as 2D or 3D games, while others are better for games that require advanced physics or AI. Understanding the needs of your game and choosing a game engine that can meet those needs is essential.

Another important factor to consider is the level of experience and expertise required to use the game engine. Some game engines are more user-friendly and require less programming knowledge, making them ideal for beginners. On the other hand, more advanced game engines may require more experience and knowledge to use effectively.

The game engine you choose can also impact the performance of your game. Some game engines are optimized for specific platforms or devices, such as iOS or Android, while others may be more versatile but may not perform as well on certain devices.

Choosing a game engine that is optimized for your target platform can help ensure your game runs smoothly and provides a great user experience.

Finally, the cost of the game engine is another important factor to consider. Some game engines are free to use, while others may require a license or subscription fee. Understanding the cost of the game engine and any associated fees is important to ensure you can stay within your budget.

In conclusion, choosing the right game engine is essential to the success of your mobile game. Understanding the needs of your game, the level of expertise required, performance optimization, and cost are all important factors to consider. Unity, Unreal, and Godot are all great game engines to consider, each with their own strengths and weaknesses.

By carefully considering all of these factors, you can choose the game engine that is right for you and your mobile game development needs.

Overview of Unity, Unreal, and Godot

When it comes to creating mobile games, choosing the right game engine is crucial. Unity, Unreal, and Godot are three of the most popular game engines available, and each one has its strengths and weaknesses. In this chapter, we'll provide an overview of each of these engines to help you determine which one is right for your mobile game development needs.

Unity

Unity is a widely-used game engine that is known for its flexibility and ease of use. It has a large community of developers and a wealth of resources available, making it an excellent choice for beginners. Unity supports a variety of platforms, including iOS and Android, and has a range of features, including built-in physics and AI tools.

One of the biggest advantages of Unity is its ability to support cross-platform development. This means that you can create a game once and then deploy it to multiple platforms without having to rewrite the code. Unity also has a user-friendly interface, making it easy to create 2D and 3D games without any prior experience.

Unreal

Unreal is another popular game engine that is known for its impressive graphics and advanced features. It is a powerful engine that is used by many AAA game developers to create high-end games. Unreal has a steep learning curve, but once you become familiar with the engine, you can create stunning mobile games with impressive graphics.

One of the main advantages of Unreal is its visual scripting system, which allows you to create complex game logic without having to write any code. Unreal also has a large community of developers and a wealth of resources available.

Godot

Godot is an open-source game engine that is gaining popularity among independent game developers. It is a lightweight engine that is easy to use and has a small learning curve. Godot supports a variety of platforms, including iOS and Android, and has a range of features, including a built-in 2D and 3D engine.

One of the biggest advantages of Godot is its flexibility. It allows you to create custom tools and workflows to suit your needs. Godot also has a small file size, making it an excellent choice for mobile game development.

Conclusion

Choosing the right game engine for your mobile game development project is essential. Unity, Unreal, and Godot each have their strengths and weaknesses, and the best choice depends on your specific needs. Unity is a good choice for beginners and supports cross-platform development. Unreal is a powerful engine with advanced features and impressive graphics.

Godot is a lightweight engine that is easy to use and flexible. Take the time to evaluate each engine and choose the one that best suits your project's requirements.

Purpose of the book

The purpose of this book is to help you find the right mobile game engine for your needs. With so many options out there, it can be overwhelming to choose between Unity, Unreal, and Godot. Each engine has its own strengths and weaknesses, and it can be difficult to know which one will work best for your project.

This book is designed to provide you with a comprehensive comparison of Unity, Unreal, and Godot. We will take an in-depth look at each engine's features, performance, ease of use, and community support.

By the end of this book, you will have a clear understanding of the pros and cons of each engine, and you will be able to make an informed decision about which one to use for your next mobile game project.

Whether you are a beginner or an experienced game developer, this book is for you. We will start with the basics of each engine and gradually work our way up to more advanced topics. You will learn how to create a simple game in each engine, and we will also cover topics such as 3D modeling, lighting, physics, and AI.

In addition to technical aspects, we will also discuss the business side of game development. We will cover topics such as monetization strategies, marketing, and community building. By the end of this book, you will have a complete understanding of what it takes to create a successful mobile game.

Overall, the purpose of this book is to provide you with the knowledge and tools you need to choose the right mobile game engine for your project. We will cover everything from the technical aspects to the business side of game development. So whether you are a solo developer or part of a team, this book will help you create the best possible mobile game.

Unity

Overview of Unity

Unity is a widely used game engine that is popular among game developers due to its user-friendly interface and powerful features. It is a cross-platform engine that allows developers to create games that can run on various platforms, including mobile devices, consoles, and desktop computers.

Unity provides a flexible and robust development environment that enables developers to create 2D and 3D games with ease. It supports scripting languages like C# and JavaScript, making it easy for developers to write code and create game logic.

Additionally, it provides a visual editor that allows developers to create game objects and adjust their properties without writing any code.

One of the significant advantages of Unity is its asset store, which provides developers with a vast collection of assets, including models, textures, and sound effects. This feature allows developers to create high-quality games in a short amount of time and at a low cost.

Unity also provides a wide range of tools for creating interactive and immersive games, including physics simulation, lighting, and animation. It also supports virtual reality (VR) and augmented reality (AR) development, making it an excellent choice for creating immersive experiences.

Unity supports various platforms, including iOS, Android, Windows, macOS, and Linux, making it an excellent choice for mobile game development. It also provides support for various game engines and platforms, including Unreal Engine and PlayStation, making it a versatile engine for game development.

In conclusion, Unity is a powerful and versatile game engine that provides developers with a flexible and robust development environment. Its asset store, visual editor, and support for multiple platforms make it an excellent choice for mobile game development.

Moreover, its support for VR and AR development makes it an excellent choice for creating immersive experiences.

Advantages of Unity

Unity, Unreal, and Godot are three of the most popular game engines used in the creation of mobile games. Each of these engines has its unique set of features and capabilities that make them suitable for different types of games. However, one of the most significant advantages of using any of these game engines is the unity they bring to the game development process.

The first advantage of unity is that it helps to streamline the game development process. Game development is a complex process that requires the collaboration of different teams, including artists, programmers, and designers. When using a game engine like Unity, all these teams can work together in one platform, which makes it easier to share assets, code, and ideas.

This saves time and reduces the risk of miscommunication, leading to a more efficient and effective game development process.

The second advantage of unity is that it allows for cross-platform development. With Unity, game developers can create games that can be played on multiple platforms, including iOS, Android, PC, and consoles. This means that the game can reach a wider audience, increasing its chances of success.

Additionally, cross-platform development saves time and resources as developers do not have to create separate versions of the game for different platforms.

The third advantage of unity is that it provides access to a vast library of assets and resources. Unity has a massive community of developers who have created a variety of assets, scripts, and plugins that can be used to enhance the game development process.

This saves time and resources as developers do not have to create everything from scratch, allowing them to focus on the core elements of the game.

Finally, unity brings a sense of community to the game development process. Game development can be a lonely and isolating process, but with Unity, developers can connect with other developers, ask for advice, and share their experiences. This creates a sense of camaraderie and support, which can help to motivate and inspire developers to create better games.

In conclusion, the unity that Unity, Unreal, and Godot bring to the game development process is an essential advantage that cannot be overlooked. From streamlining game development to providing access to a vast library of assets and resources, unity is a crucial factor in creating successful mobile games.

User-friendly interface

User-friendly interface is one of the most important aspects of any mobile game engine. It is the first thing that a user interacts with, and it sets the tone for the entire game development process. A user-friendly interface ensures that game developers can easily navigate the software, understand its features, and make changes without too much hassle.

When it comes to mobile game engines, Unity, Unreal, and Godot all have user-friendly interfaces, but they differ in terms of their ease of use.

Unity is known for its intuitive user interface, which is easy to navigate for developers of all skill levels. The engine has a drag-and-drop interface, which allows users to simply drag assets from the library and drop them into the scene. This makes it easy to create complex scenes without writing any code.

Additionally, Unity has a visual scripting system, which allows users to create game logic without writing any code.

Unreal, on the other hand, has a more complex user interface compared to Unity. While it is still intuitive and easy to navigate, it requires more effort to learn. Unreal uses a node-based system, which can be overwhelming for new users. However, once users get the hang of it, they find it to be incredibly powerful and efficient.

Godot, like Unity, has a straightforward user interface that is easy to navigate. The engine uses a node-based system that is similar to Unreal, but it is less overwhelming for new users. Additionally, Godot has a visual scripting system that allows users to create game logic without writing any code.

In conclusion, all three mobile game engines have user-friendly interfaces, but Unity is the most intuitive and easy to use. Unreal has a more complex interface, but it is incredibly powerful and efficient once users get the hang of it. Godot is similar to Unity in terms of ease of use, but it has a few extra features that make it stand out.

Ultimately, the choice of mobile game engine will depend on the user's skill level and the complexity of the game they want to create.

Large community support

One of the essential factors to consider when selecting a mobile game engine is the availability of a large community. The community of a game engine is a group of developers, designers, and enthusiasts who share their knowledge, resources, and feedback to improve the engine and help others.

Unity, Unreal, and Godot have a considerable community of users and contributors worldwide. These communities offer a vast range of benefits to game developers, including free tutorials, assets, plugins, forums, and support. They also help to solve problems, provide feedback, and give suggestions on how to optimize the performance of the game engine.

Unity, which is the most popular mobile game engine, has a massive community of users and contributors. The Unity community has over 2 million developers worldwide, and it is constantly growing. Unity Connect is a platform where Unity users can share their work, collaborate, and get feedback from other developers.

Unity also has a forum where users can get help, share tips and tricks, and find solutions to their problems.

Unreal Engine also has a large community of users and contributors. The Unreal community has over 7 million developers worldwide, and it is one of the most active game engine communities. Unreal has a forum where users can ask questions, share their work, and get feedback. It also has a marketplace where developers can buy or sell assets, plugins, and tools.

Godot, although not as popular as Unity and Unreal, has a growing community of users and contributors. The Godot community has over 300,000 developers worldwide, and it is constantly expanding. Godot has a forum where users can ask questions, share their work, and get feedback. It also has a community-driven documentation that is regularly updated.

In conclusion, having a large community of users and contributors is a significant advantage when selecting a mobile game engine. The community offers free resources, support, feedback, and solutions to problems. Unity, Unreal, and Godot have a considerable community of users and contributors that make them great choices for mobile game development.

Cross-platform development

Cross-platform development is one of the most important aspects of mobile game development. It allows you to create a game that can be played on multiple platforms, including iOS, Android, and PC, without having to create separate versions for each platform. This makes development faster, more efficient, and ultimately saves you time and money.

Unity, Unreal, and Godot all offer cross-platform development as a standard feature. With Unity, you can develop games for over 25 different platforms, including mobile, desktop, and console. Unreal Engine also supports multiple platforms, including iOS, Android, and PC, and offers a range of tools and features to make cross-platform development easier.

Godot, on the other hand, is a more lightweight engine that supports cross-platform development for mobile, desktop, and web.

When it comes to cross-platform development, one of the most important factors to consider is the programming language used by the engine. Unity uses C#, which is a popular and widely-used language that is easy to learn and work with.

Unreal Engine, on the other hand, uses C++, which is a more complex and powerful language that can be more difficult to master but offers more control and flexibility. Godot uses its own scripting language, GDScript, which is similar to Python and is easy to learn and use.

Another important factor to consider when developing cross-platform games is the user interface (UI) and user experience (UX). Each platform has its own unique UI and UX guidelines, and it's important to ensure that your game meets these guidelines to provide the best possible experience for users.

Unity, Unreal, and Godot all offer tools and features to help you create a consistent and seamless UI and UX across multiple platforms.

In conclusion, cross-platform development is a vital aspect of mobile game development, and Unity, Unreal, and Godot all offer robust tools and features to make cross-platform development easier and more efficient.

When choosing an engine for your next mobile game project, be sure to consider the programming language, UI/UX tools, and platform support to ensure that your game is a success on all platforms.

Disadvantages of Unity

As with anything, there are both advantages and disadvantages to using Unity as a mobile game engine. While Unity has become a very popular engine in recent years, it's important to consider some of the potential downsides that come with using it.

One of the biggest disadvantages of Unity is its cost. While the engine does offer a free version, many of the more advanced features require a paid license. This can be a significant cost for indie developers or small studios, especially when compared to the free options offered by other engines like Godot.

Another potential disadvantage of Unity is its steep learning curve. While the engine does offer a lot of documentation and tutorials, it can still be quite challenging for beginners to get started with. This can be particularly frustrating for developers who are looking to quickly prototype and iterate on their game ideas.

Unity also has a reputation for being resource-intensive, particularly when it comes to memory usage. This can be a problem for mobile devices, which often have limited hardware capabilities. Developers need to be careful not to overload their games with too many assets or complex scripts, or risk causing performance issues on lower-end devices.

Finally, Unity's scripting language, C#, can be a barrier for developers who are more comfortable with other programming languages. While C# is a powerful language with a lot of features, it can take some time to learn and get comfortable with.

While these may seem like significant disadvantages, it's important to remember that Unity is still a powerful and flexible engine that can be used to create a wide variety of games. Ultimately, whether or not Unity is the right choice for your project will depend on your specific needs and goals as a developer.

High learning curve

When it comes to game development, there's always a learning curve. However, some engines have a steeper curve than others. Unity, Unreal, and Godot each have their own unique challenges when it comes to learning the ins and outs of the engine.

Unity is often considered a great choice for beginners because it has a relatively low learning curve. The interface is user-friendly, and there are plenty of tutorials and resources available to help new developers get started. However, as you move beyond the basics, Unity can become quite complex. There are many advanced features and techniques that can take time to master.

Additionally, Unity's scripting language, C#, can be difficult for those without programming experience.

Unreal, on the other hand, has a reputation for having a high learning curve. The engine is more complex than Unity, and the interface can be overwhelming for new developers. However, once you get past the initial hurdle, Unreal is incredibly powerful. The engine's visual scripting language, Blueprint, makes it easy to create complex gameplay systems without needing to write any code.

However, if you do want to write code, Unreal uses C++, which can be challenging for beginners.

Godot falls somewhere in between Unity and Unreal when it comes to the learning curve. The engine is relatively easy to use, with a straightforward interface and plenty of documentation. However, Godot's scripting language, GDScript, can take some time to get used to.

Additionally, because Godot is a newer engine, there aren't as many resources available as there are for Unity and Unreal.

In the end, the learning curve for each engine will depend on your experience level and what you're trying to accomplish. If you're a beginner, Unity is likely the best choice. If you're looking for more power and are willing to put in the time to learn, Unreal may be the way to go. And if you're looking for a middle ground, Godot could be a great option.

Regardless of which engine you choose, remember that game development is a marathon, not a sprint. Take the time to learn the engine and develop your skills, and you'll be well on your way to creating great games.

Limited graphics capabilities

Limited graphics capabilities can be a significant issue when it comes to mobile game development. Since mobile devices often have lower processing power and memory compared to desktop computers, developers may face limitations when it comes to creating high-quality graphics for their games.

Unity, Unreal, and Godot are all powerful game engines that have their own strengths and weaknesses when it comes to graphics capabilities. However, it is important to note that even the most advanced game engines will not be able to overcome the hardware limitations of mobile devices.

That being said, Unity has a reputation for being beginner-friendly and offering a range of tools and features for developing games with 2D and 3D graphics. The engine has a built-in graphics editor, which allows developers to create and modify assets directly within the game engine.

Unreal, on the other hand, is known for its advanced graphics capabilities, including its powerful rendering engine and support for high-end graphics features such as dynamic lighting and real-time reflections.

However, this level of graphical fidelity may not be feasible for all mobile devices, and developers may need to optimize their games to run smoothly on lower-end devices.

Godot, while not as well-known as Unity and Unreal, is a free and open-source game engine that offers a range of features for 2D and 3D game development. While it may not have the same level of advanced graphics capabilities as Unreal, Godot is still a powerful engine that can be used to create high-quality games for mobile devices.

Ultimately, the choice of game engine will depend on the specific needs and goals of each individual developer. While graphics capabilities are certainly an important consideration, other factors such as ease of use, community support, and cost may also play a role in the decision-making process.

By carefully weighing the pros and cons of each engine, developers can choose the one that best suits their needs and creates the best possible gaming experience for their audience.

Expensive pricing model

Expensive Pricing Model

One of the biggest concerns for game developers is the cost of using a game engine. The pricing models for Unity, Unreal, and Godot differ significantly, and it is essential to understand how each one works to make an informed decision.

Unity offers a subscription-based model that starts at $35 per month for the basic plan, which includes access to all core engine features, 2D and 3D game development tools, and support for PC, Mac, and Linux platforms. For larger teams or studios, Unity offers a pro plan that starts at $125 per month, which includes additional features such as priority support, cloud-based services, and analytics tools.

Unreal, on the other hand, offers a royalty-based model, meaning that developers pay a percentage of their game's revenue to Epic Games, the company behind Unreal. The royalty percentage starts at 5% but can be negotiated for larger projects.

Unreal also offers a subscription-based model, which includes access to all engine features, source code, and support for various platforms, starting at $19 per month.

Godot, unlike Unity and Unreal, is entirely free and open-source, meaning that developers can use it for any purpose, including commercial projects, without paying any fees. The engine is also community-driven, meaning that developers can contribute to its development and share their knowledge with others.

While Unity and Unreal's pricing models may seem expensive, they offer a range of features and support that can help developers create high-quality games. However, for smaller developers or those on a tight budget, Godot may be a more attractive option due to its free and open-source nature.

In conclusion, the pricing models for Unity, Unreal, and Godot differ significantly, and it is essential to understand how each one works before choosing a mobile game engine. While Unity and Unreal's subscription and royalty-based models may seem expensive, they offer a range of features and support that can help developers create high-quality games.

However, for smaller developers or those on a tight budget, Godot may be a more attractive option due to its free and open-source nature.

Case studies

In the world of game development, case studies are essential tools that can help developers understand the strengths and weaknesses of different game engines. In this chapter, we will take a closer look at some case studies that compare the performance of Unity, Unreal, and Godot.

Case Study 1: Unity vs Unreal

In 2018, a team of developers from 3DRealms set out to create a new first-person shooter game called Ion Maiden. The team had to decide which game engine to use, and ultimately chose to work with Unreal. They cited Unreal's superior graphics capabilities and the ability to create complex environments as the main reasons for their choice.

However, the team also noted that Unreal's learning curve was steep, and that it took some time to get used to the engine's workflow. They also found that Unreal's licensing fees were higher than Unity's. Despite these challenges, the team was able to create a visually stunning game that received critical acclaim upon release.

Case Study 2: Godot vs Unity

In 2019, a team of developers from Studio Wildcard set out to create a mobile game based on their hit PC game, ARK: Survival Evolved. The team initially chose to work with Unity, but after encountering performance issues on mobile devices, they switched to Godot.

The team found that Godot was more lightweight and performed better on mobile devices than Unity. They also found that Godot's scripting language was easier to work with than Unity's C# scripting language. However, the team noted that Godot's documentation was not as comprehensive as Unity's, which made it more challenging to learn the engine.

Despite these challenges, the team was able to create a successful mobile game that received positive reviews from players.

Case Study 3: Unity vs Godot

In 2020, a team of developers from Blackbird Interactive set out to create a real-time strategy game called Homeworld 3. The team initially chose to work with Unity but switched to Godot after encountering performance issues.

The team found that Godot was faster and more lightweight than Unity, which allowed them to create more complex environments and gameplay mechanics without sacrificing performance. They also found that Godot's node-based workflow was easier to work with than Unity's component-based workflow.

However, the team noted that Godot's lack of a visual scripting system made it more challenging to prototype gameplay mechanics.

Despite these challenges, the team was able to create a visually stunning game that received critical acclaim upon release.

Conclusion:

These case studies demonstrate that each game engine has its strengths and weaknesses, and that the choice of engine ultimately depends on the needs of the project. Unity is a robust engine that is well-suited for creating complex games, while Unreal is ideal for creating visually stunning games with complex environments.

Godot is lightweight and performs well on mobile devices, making it an excellent choice for mobile game development. By understanding the strengths and weaknesses of each engine, developers can make informed decisions about which engine to use for their projects.

Pokémon Go

Pokémon Go took the world by storm in 2016, becoming one of the most popular mobile games of all time. It was the first augmented reality (AR) game to make such a huge impact, and it was a major milestone for the gaming industry.

The game was developed by Niantic, Inc. and was released on July 6, 2016, for iOS and Android devices. It was an instant hit, with millions of downloads within the first few days of its release.

Pokémon Go is an AR game that allows players to catch virtual Pokémon in real-world locations. It uses the player's GPS and camera to create an immersive gaming experience. The game allows players to explore their surroundings, catch Pokémon, and battle other players in gyms.

Pokémon Go was developed using the Unity game engine. Unity is a popular game engine that is known for its ease of use and flexibility. It is used by many developers to create mobile and PC games.

The Unity game engine allowed Niantic to create a seamless AR experience for players. The engine has built-in support for AR, which made it easier for Niantic to develop the game. It also provided the tools needed to create a multiplayer gaming experience, which is an essential part of Pokémon Go.

Unity is a cross-platform game engine, which means that it can be used to develop games for multiple platforms, including iOS, Android, and PC. This was an important factor for Niantic, as they wanted to reach as many players as possible.

Pokémon Go has been a huge success, and it has paved the way for other AR games. It has also shown the power of the Unity game engine, and how it can be used to create immersive gaming experiences.

Angry Birds

Angry Birds is a game that has been played by millions of people around the world. It is a mobile game that has become so popular that it has spawned a franchise of movies, merchandise, and even theme parks. But what makes this game so special? And how does it fit into the world of mobile game engines?

At its core, Angry Birds is a physics-based puzzle game. Players launch birds at structures that are populated by pigs. The goal is to destroy the structures and eliminate the pigs. The game uses simple mechanics, but it is challenging and addictive. As players progress through the levels, they encounter new obstacles and challenges.

So, where does Angry Birds fit into the world of mobile game engines? The game was developed using the Unity engine. Unity is a popular choice for mobile game developers because it is easy to use, has a large community of developers, and is compatible with multiple platforms.

Unity provides developers with a range of tools and features that make it easy to create physics-based games like Angry Birds. The engine has a built-in physics engine, which means that developers don't need to write their own physics code. This saves time and makes it easier to create realistic physics-based effects.

In addition to the physics engine, Unity also provides developers with a range of other tools and features that make it easy to create mobile games. These include graphics, audio, and animation tools, as well as support for multiple platforms.

One of the key benefits of using Unity for mobile game development is its cross-platform support. Unity supports iOS, Android, and other mobile platforms, which means that developers can create games that can be played on multiple devices. This makes it easier to reach a wider audience and potentially increase revenue.

In conclusion, Angry Birds is a game that has captured the hearts of millions of people around the world. It is an excellent example of a physics-based puzzle game, and it was developed using the Unity game engine.

Unity provides developers with a range of tools and features that make it easy to create mobile games, and its cross-platform support makes it an excellent choice for mobile game development.

Temple Run

Temple Run is one of the most popular mobile games of all time, and it's a great example of what can be achieved with the right game engine. If you're looking to create a game like Temple Run, you'll need to choose the right mobile game engine to make it happen.

Unity, Unreal, and Godot are all popular choices for mobile game development, but which one is right for you? Let's take a closer look at each game engine and see how they stack up when it comes to creating a game like Temple Run.

Unity is a popular game engine that's used by many mobile game developers. It's known for its ease of use and its ability to create games quickly. With Unity, you can create 2D and 3D games, and there are plenty of resources available to help you get started. However, Unity can be limited in terms of the graphics and the complexity of the game you can create.

Unreal is another popular game engine that's known for its high-quality graphics and its ability to create complex games. If you're looking to create a game like Temple Run that's visually stunning and has a lot of moving parts, then Unreal might be the right choice for you. However, Unreal can be more difficult to learn than other game engines, and it can be more resource-intensive.

Godot is a newer game engine that's gaining popularity among mobile game developers. It's open source, which means it's free to use, and it's known for its ease of use and its ability to create 2D and 3D games. With Godot, you can create games quickly and easily, and there are plenty of resources available to help you get started.

However, Godot is still a relatively new game engine, and it may not have all of the features you need to create a game like Temple Run.

In conclusion, when it comes to creating a game like Temple Run, the right game engine for you will depend on your specific needs and preferences. Unity is a great choice if you're looking for an easy-to-use game engine that can create games quickly. Unreal is a good choice if you're looking for high-quality graphics and the ability to create complex games.

Godot is a good choice if you're looking for a free, easy-to-use game engine that can create 2D and 3D games. No matter which game engine you choose, with the right tools and resources, you can create a game like Temple Run that's fun, engaging, and visually stunning.

Unreal

Overview of Unreal

Overview of Unreal

Unreal is one of the most popular mobile game engines available today, alongside Unity and Godot. It is a powerful game engine designed to create high-quality games that run smoothly on different platforms. It was developed by Epic Games, the same company behind popular games like Fortnite and Gears of War.

Unreal is known for its advanced graphics capabilities, making it a popular choice for developers who want to create visually stunning games. It also offers a wide range of features and tools that allow developers to create complex game mechanics and gameplay systems.

One of the key strengths of Unreal is its Blueprint system, which allows developers to create game logic and mechanics without the need for coding. This makes it easier for non-programmers to get started with game development and create prototypes quickly. However, for more complex game mechanics and systems, coding may still be necessary.

Unreal also boasts an active community of developers who create and share plugins and extensions that enhance the engine's capabilities. These plugins can range from simple tools that streamline workflows to more advanced features like AI and physics simulations.

In terms of platform support, Unreal is compatible with a wide range of platforms, including PC, Mac, iOS, Android, and consoles like PlayStation and Xbox. This makes it a versatile choice for developers who want to create games for multiple platforms.

Overall, Unreal is a powerful game engine that offers advanced graphics capabilities, a wide range of features and tools, and strong community support. It is a popular choice for developers who want to create visually stunning games that run smoothly on different platforms.

Advantages of Unreal

Unreal Engine, developed by Epic Games, is a popular game engine used for creating high-quality 3D games for various platforms, including PC, console, VR, and mobile. While Unity and Godot are popular game engines, Unreal has several advantages that make it stand out from the competition.

One of the major advantages of Unreal is its visual scripting language, Blueprint. Blueprint allows developers to create game logic and behaviors visually, without needing to write code. This makes game development more accessible to designers and artists who may not have programming experience.

Blueprint also has a node-based interface that allows developers to easily connect inputs and outputs, making it easy to create complex systems and AI.

Another advantage of Unreal is its advanced graphics capabilities. The engine has a powerful rendering system that supports real-time ray tracing, dynamic lighting, and advanced post-processing effects. This allows developers to create stunning visuals and realistic environments for their games. Additionally, Unreal supports high-end graphics features such as HDR, bloom, depth of field, and motion blur.

Unreal also has a strong community and extensive documentation. The engine has been used to create some of the most successful and popular games in recent years, including Fortnite, Gears of War, and Batman: Arkham Knight. The Unreal community is active and supportive, with many resources available online for learning and troubleshooting.

Finally, Unreal has strong support for virtual reality (VR) and augmented reality (AR) development. The engine has built-in support for popular VR headsets such as Oculus Rift and HTC Vive, as well as AR platforms such as ARKit and ARCore. This makes it easy for developers to create immersive VR and AR experiences for their games.

In conclusion, Unreal Engine offers several advantages for game developers, including its visual scripting language, advanced graphics capabilities, strong community, extensive documentation, and support for VR and AR development.

While Unity and Godot are also popular game engines, Unreal is the clear choice for developers who want to create high-quality, visually stunning games that push the boundaries of what is possible in game development.

High-end graphics capabilities

High-end graphics capabilities are essential when it comes to developing mobile games. When gamers download a mobile game, they expect to see high-quality graphics that will keep them engaged for hours. This is where choosing the right mobile game engine becomes crucial.

Unity, Unreal, and Godot are all known for their high-end graphics capabilities, but each has its unique features that make them stand out. Unity, for instance, is known for its ease of use and support for 2D and 3D graphics. Unreal, on the other hand, is known for its photorealistic graphics that can rival those of high-end PC games.

Godot, on the other hand, is known for its flexibility and support for a wide range of platforms.

When it comes to high-end graphics, Unity is a popular choice for mobile game developers. Its graphics engine is designed to optimize graphics performance, making it possible to create visually stunning games without compromising performance. Unity also supports advanced graphics features such as real-time lighting, particle systems, and post-processing effects.

Unreal, on the other hand, is known for its ability to create photorealistic graphics that are unmatched in the mobile gaming industry. The engine supports advanced graphics features such as dynamic lighting, advanced shading, and real-time global illumination. These features make it possible to create games with stunning visuals that can rival those of high-end PC games.

Godot, while not as well-known as Unity and Unreal, is gaining popularity among mobile game developers for its flexibility and support for a wide range of platforms. The engine supports both 2D and 3D graphics and has an intuitive interface that makes it easy to create games with stunning visuals.

In conclusion, high-end graphics capabilities are crucial when it comes to developing mobile games. Unity, Unreal, and Godot all have their unique features that make them stand out in this area. Whether you are looking for ease of use, photorealistic graphics or flexibility, there is a mobile game engine that will meet your needs.

It is up to you to decide which one is right for your game development needs.

Robust engine features

When it comes to developing mobile games, having a robust engine is crucial. A robust engine means that the game is optimized, runs smoothly, and can handle a lot of data without crashing. In this subchapter, we will explore the robust engine features of Unity, Unreal, and Godot and how they can benefit mobile game developers.

Unity is known for its robust engine features, which allow developers to create complex games with ease. One of the most significant features of Unity is its ability to handle large amounts of data. This makes it ideal for developing games that require a lot of assets and animations. Unity also has a powerful physics engine that allows developers to create realistic simulations of objects and environments.

Unreal is another engine that has robust features, making it a popular choice for mobile game development. Unreal's engine is known for its ability to handle complex graphics and create high-quality visual effects. It also has a powerful physics engine that allows developers to create realistic simulations of objects and environments.

Godot is a newer engine but has quickly gained popularity among game developers. Its robust engine features allow developers to create games with ease. One of the most significant features of Godot is its ability to create 2D and 3D games with ease. It also has a powerful physics engine that allows developers to create realistic simulations of objects and environments.

Overall, when it comes to choosing a mobile game engine, it is essential to consider the robust engine features. Unity, Unreal, and Godot all have their unique features that make them ideal for mobile game development. However, it ultimately comes down to the needs of the game and the preferences of the developer.

The best way to determine which engine is right for you is to try each one out and see which one works best for you.

Accessible source code

Accessible source code is a crucial aspect of game development, especially for those who are new to game development or those who want to make modifications to the game engine they are using. In this subchapter, we will discuss what accessible source code means, and how it affects game development in Unity, Unreal, and Godot.

Accessible source code refers to the ability to access and modify the source code of the game engine. This means that developers can make changes to the underlying code of the engine, allowing them to customize the engine to fit their specific needs. Accessible source code also enables developers to fix bugs, add new features, and optimize performance.

Unity, Unreal, and Godot all have accessible source code, but there are differences in how they approach this aspect of game development. Unity provides its source code for free, but developers are not allowed to modify or distribute it. Unreal, on the other hand, provides full access to its source code, allowing developers to modify it as they see fit.

Godot also provides its source code for free and allows developers to modify and distribute it.

The accessibility of source code has a significant impact on the development process. For example, having access to the source code can make it easier to debug issues and optimize performance. It also enables developers to add new features to the engine, which can be a significant advantage over competitors.

However, accessible source code also comes with challenges. Modifying source code can be time-consuming and requires a strong understanding of programming languages. Additionally, modifying the code can make it more difficult to update the engine in the future.

Ultimately, the decision to use a game engine with accessible source code comes down to the specific needs of the project. Unity is a great option for those who want a user-friendly engine with accessible source code, but are not interested in modifying it. Unreal is a good choice for those who want full access to the source code and are comfortable with modifying it.

Godot is a great option for those who want a free engine with accessible source code and a strong community of developers.

In conclusion, accessible source code is an essential aspect of game development, and it is important to consider this factor when choosing a game engine. Each engine has its approach to accessible source code, and choosing the right engine for your project depends on your specific needs and preferences.

Disadvantages of Unreal

While Unreal is one of the most popular game engines out there, it's not without its drawbacks. Here are some of the disadvantages of using Unreal for mobile game development:

1. Steep learning curve: Unreal is known for being a complex engine, with a lot of features and tools that can be overwhelming for beginners. If you're new to game development, you may find it difficult to get started with Unreal compared to other engines.

2. Resource-intensive: Unreal is a powerful engine, but that power comes at a cost. It requires a lot of resources to run, which can be a problem for mobile devices with limited processing power and memory. This can result in lower performance and longer load times, which can be frustrating for players.

3. Limited mobile support: While Unreal does have mobile support, it's not as robust as other engines like Unity. This means that you may run into more issues when developing for mobile devices, and you may need to do more optimization work to get your game running smoothly.

4. Licensing fees: Unlike Unity and Godot, Unreal requires developers to pay a licensing fee to use the engine. This can be a significant expense, especially for indie developers or small studios with limited budgets.

5. Limited asset store: Unreal's asset store is not as extensive as Unity's, which means that you may have to create more assets from scratch or pay for custom assets. This can be time-consuming and expensive, and may limit the scope of your game.

While Unreal is a powerful engine with a lot of features, it may not be the best choice for everyone. If you're new to game development or working on a mobile game with limited resources, you may want to consider other options like Unity or Godot.

However, if you're an experienced developer with a larger budget and a need for advanced features, Unreal may be the right choice for you.

Steep learning curve

The world of mobile game development can be overwhelming, especially when it comes to choosing the right game engine. Unity, Unreal, and Godot are three of the most popular game engines on the market, but each comes with its own unique set of features and challenges.

One of the biggest challenges that developers face when starting out with any of these engines is the steep learning curve. While all three engines offer user-friendly interfaces and extensive documentation, the sheer amount of information to absorb can be daunting.

Unity, for example, has a vast library of tools and features that can take months to master. From scripting with C# to creating complex animations and physics simulations, there is no shortage of learning opportunities. Unreal, on the other hand, has a steeper learning curve due to its more complex architecture.

With a focus on high-end graphics and immersive experiences, Unreal requires a deeper understanding of programming and game design principles.

Godot, while more accessible than Unreal, still requires a significant investment of time and effort to master. With its unique node-based approach to scene creation and scripting, Godot can be challenging for those accustomed to more traditional game engines.

However, the time and effort invested in learning these engines can pay off in spades. With their powerful toolsets and flexibility, Unity, Unreal, and Godot offer developers the ability to create truly stunning mobile games. From immersive 3D environments to realistic physics simulations, the possibilities are endless.

Ultimately, the key to overcoming the steep learning curve is to take things one step at a time. Start with the basics and work your way up, taking advantage of the extensive documentation and online resources available for each engine. With patience and persistence, any developer can master Unity, Unreal, or Godot and create mobile games that stand out from the crowd.

Limited cross-platform development

Limited cross-platform development is a common issue that mobile game developers encounter when using Unity, Unreal, and Godot engines. Although these game engines offer cross-platform development features, limitations exist that prevent developers from achieving true cross-platform compatibility.

One of the most significant challenges is the difference in programming languages used by each engine. Unity uses C# while Unreal uses C++, which causes compatibility issues with platforms that do not support these languages. Godot, on the other hand, uses its own scripting language, GDScript, which limits the compatibility of the engine with other platforms.

Another challenge is the difference in operating systems and hardware between platforms. While Unity and Unreal support a wide range of platforms, including Windows, macOS, iOS, Android, and consoles like Xbox and PlayStation, Godot has limited support for platforms beyond Windows and macOS.

Additionally, even with cross-platform development, developers need to consider the differences in screen sizes, input methods, and performance capabilities of each platform they target. This means that developers need to tailor their game design to suit the limitations of each platform, taking extra time and effort to ensure that the game works seamlessly across all platforms.

Despite these limitations, cross-platform development remains a valuable feature for game developers, allowing them to reach a wider audience and increase their revenue potential.

By leveraging the cross-platform development features of Unity, Unreal, and Godot, developers can create games that work across multiple platforms and devices, reducing development costs and increasing efficiency.

In conclusion, limited cross-platform development is a challenge that many mobile game developers face when working with Unity, Unreal, and Godot engines.

However, with careful consideration of the differences in programming languages, operating systems, and hardware, developers can overcome these limitations and create games that work seamlessly across multiple platforms.

Expensive pricing model

One of the biggest challenges for game developers is determining the right pricing model for their mobile games. Unfortunately, some game engines offer an expensive pricing model that can be difficult for developers to manage.

Unity, Unreal, and Godot are all popular game engines that offer various pricing models to developers. However, some of these models can be costly and may not be suitable for every developer. For instance, Unity's pricing model can be quite expensive, especially for developers who are just starting out.

Unity offers three pricing tiers: Personal, Plus, and Pro. The Personal tier is free and offers basic features, but the Plus and Pro tiers can cost from $35/month to $125/month. This can be a significant expense for small developers who are still trying to generate revenue from their games.

Similarly, Unreal Engine offers a subscription-based model with a cost of $19/month plus a 5% royalty fee. While this pricing model can be affordable for some developers, it can also be a significant expense for others.

Godot, on the other hand, offers a completely free and open-source game engine that can be downloaded and used by anyone. This makes it an ideal choice for developers who are just starting out or who are working on a tight budget.

It's important for developers to carefully consider the cost of the game engine they choose to use. While Unity and Unreal may offer advanced features, the cost may be too high for some developers. Godot, on the other hand, offers a free and open-source option that can be a great choice for developers who want to keep their expenses low.

Ultimately, the decision of which game engine to use will depend on each developer's unique situation. It's important to carefully evaluate the features and pricing of each engine before making a decision. By doing so, developers can choose the best engine for their needs and budget, and create amazing mobile games that their players will love.

Case studies

Case studies are an excellent way to understand how game developers utilize different mobile game engines. In this chapter, we will explore some case studies of games developed using Unity, Unreal, and Godot.

Case Study 1: Crossy Road

Crossy Road is a popular mobile game developed by Hipster Whale, an Australian game development company. The game was initially developed using Unity3D and has since been ported to other platforms. The game is a simple but addictive endless runner where the player controls a character trying to cross a busy road.

The game has simple 3D graphics and was designed to be accessible to players of all ages. The game's success can be attributed to its simple gameplay, charming graphics, and accessibility.

Case Study 2: Fortnite

Fortnite is an incredibly popular battle royale game developed by Epic Games. The game was initially developed using Unreal Engine 4 and has since become one of the most popular games in the world. The game's success can be attributed to its unique gameplay, excellent graphics, and constant updates.

The game's development team was able to utilize the power of Unreal Engine 4 to create a game with stunning visuals and smooth gameplay.

Case Study 3: SuperTuxKart

SuperTuxKart is an open-source racing game developed using Godot Engine. The game features cute characters, colorful graphics, and fun gameplay. The game's development team was able to utilize Godot's features to create a game with smooth gameplay and excellent graphics.

The game's open-source nature has allowed it to attract a dedicated fan base that has helped to improve the game's features and gameplay.

Conclusion

Case studies are an excellent way to understand how different game engines can be utilized to create unique and engaging games. Unity, Unreal, and Godot are all great game engines that can be used to create games of varying complexity and styles. The choice of engine ultimately depends on the game's requirements, budget, and development team's skills.

By understanding how other developers have utilized these engines, game developers can make informed decisions when choosing the right engine for their projects.

Fortnite

Fortnite is a massively popular multiplayer online game that has taken the gaming world by storm. Developed by Epic Games, Fortnite has become a cultural phenomenon that has transcended the world of gaming and entered mainstream popular culture. It is one of the most successful games of all time, with over 350 million registered players worldwide.

Fortnite is a battle royale game that pits up to 100 players against each other in a fight to be the last one standing. The game is set on an island in which players must scavenge for weapons, resources, and other items to survive. As the game progresses, the playable area of the island becomes smaller and smaller, forcing players into closer and more intense combat.

One of the reasons why Fortnite has become so popular is its accessibility. The game is free to play and can be downloaded on multiple platforms, including PC, PlayStation, Xbox, and mobile devices. This has allowed a wide range of players to enjoy the game, from hardcore gamers to casual players who may be new to the world of gaming.

Fortnite is also known for its unique aesthetic, with colorful graphics and a playful tone. This has helped to attract a younger audience, who have become some of the game's most dedicated players. The game also features a variety of in-game events and challenges that keep players engaged and coming back for more.

From a development standpoint, Fortnite was built using Unreal Engine 4, which is one of the most powerful game engines available. This has allowed Epic Games to create a game that is visually stunning and runs smoothly on a wide range of devices. The use of Unreal Engine 4 has also made it easier for Epic Games to release updates and new content for the game.

Overall, Fortnite is a game that has made a huge impact on the gaming world and beyond. Its accessibility, unique aesthetic, and use of powerful game engine technology have all contributed to its success.

If you're interested in developing a game that can capture the same level of excitement and engagement as Fortnite, it's worth considering using a powerful game engine like Unreal Engine 4.

PUBG Mobile

PUBG Mobile is one of the most popular mobile games in the world, and for good reason. The game offers a unique blend of battle royale gameplay and realistic graphics, making it highly addictive and enjoyable for players of all skill levels.

Developed by Tencent Games, PUBG Mobile is based on the original PC version of the game, which was released in 2017. The mobile version of the game was released in 2018 and quickly became one of the most downloaded games on both iOS and Android.

One of the key features of PUBG Mobile is its realistic graphics. The game uses the Unreal Engine 4, which is known for its high-quality visuals and realistic physics. This means that players can experience a highly immersive gameplay experience, with detailed environments and realistic player movements.

In addition to its graphics, PUBG Mobile also offers a variety of gameplay modes, including classic battle royale, arcade mode, and sniper training. Each mode offers a unique challenge and requires players to use different strategies to win.

While PUBG Mobile is a highly enjoyable game, it does have some drawbacks. One of the biggest issues with the game is its large file size, which can take up a significant amount of storage space on a mobile device. Additionally, the game can be quite demanding on a device's hardware, which can lead to lag and other performance issues.

Despite these drawbacks, PUBG Mobile remains one of the most popular mobile games in the world. With its realistic graphics, engaging gameplay, and variety of modes, it offers a highly enjoyable gaming experience for players of all skill levels.

If you're looking for a mobile game engine that can create a similar experience to PUBG Mobile, Unreal Engine 4 is a great choice. With its advanced graphics capabilities and realistic physics, it can create highly immersive environments that rival those of PUBG Mobile. However, if you're looking for a more lightweight engine that can run on lower-end devices, Godot may be a better choice.

Ultimately, the choice of engine will depend on your specific needs and preferences.

Asphalt 9: Legends

Asphalt 9: Legends is a popular racing game that has taken the mobile gaming world by storm. Developed by Gameloft, this game is all about high-speed racing, slick graphics, and intense gameplay. But what makes Asphalt 9: Legends stand out from other racing games? And how does it stack up against other popular mobile game engines like Unity, Unreal, and Godot?

One of the standout features of Asphalt 9: Legends is its stunning graphics. The game features high-quality visuals that make every race feel like a cinematic experience. The cars look sleek and shiny, the environments are detailed and dynamic, and the special effects add an extra layer of excitement to the game.

The gameplay is also top-notch, with intuitive controls that make it easy to navigate through tight turns and avoid obstacles. The game offers a variety of different modes, including a career mode where you can unlock new cars and tracks as you progress, and a multiplayer mode where you can compete against other players from around the world.

But how does Asphalt 9: Legends compare to other mobile game engines like Unity, Unreal, and Godot? In terms of graphics, Asphalt 9: Legends is on par with Unity and Unreal, both of which are known for their high-quality visuals. However, Godot falls short in this area, as it is not as advanced as the other two engines.

When it comes to gameplay, Asphalt 9: Legends holds its own against Unity and Unreal, both of which are known for their flexible and powerful game engines. Godot, on the other hand, is still a relatively new player in the mobile game engine market and may not offer the same level of customization and flexibility as the other two engines.

Overall, Asphalt 9: Legends is a fantastic game that showcases the power and potential of modern mobile game engines. Whether you're a fan of racing games or just looking for a fun and engaging mobile gaming experience, Asphalt 9: Legends is definitely worth checking out.

And if you're interested in developing your own mobile games, be sure to consider the strengths and weaknesses of different game engines like Unity, Unreal, and Godot to find the one that is right for you.

Godot

Overview of Godot

Overview of Godot

Godot is a free and open-source game engine that offers a wide range of features and tools for game development. It is a popular choice among developers who want to create 2D and 3D games for desktop, mobile, and web platforms.

One of the key features of Godot is its visual scripting system, which allows developers to create complex game logic without writing any code. This makes it an ideal choice for beginners who are new to game development.

Another advantage of Godot is its versatility. It supports multiple programming languages, including C#, Python, and GDScript, which is a high-level scripting language specifically designed for game development in Godot. This makes it easy for developers to work with their preferred language and tools.

Godot also offers a wide range of built-in tools and resources, including a robust physics engine, audio and video playback, and animation tools. It also includes a powerful 2D and 3D editor, which allows developers to create and edit game assets directly within the engine.

In addition, Godot is known for its performance, with a lightweight and efficient architecture that allows for fast and smooth gameplay. This makes it a popular choice among developers who want to create games for mobile platforms, where performance is critical.

Overall, Godot is a powerful and versatile game engine that offers a wide range of features and tools for game development. Whether you are a beginner or an experienced developer, Godot has something to offer, making it a worthy competitor to Unity and Unreal in the mobile game engine market.

Advantages of Godot

When it comes to choosing a mobile game engine, there are a few options that stand out among the rest. Unity and Unreal are two of the most popular, but there's another contender that's worth considering: Godot.

Godot is an open-source game engine that provides developers with a powerful set of tools for creating 2D and 3D games. It has gained a lot of popularity over the years, and for good reason. Here are some of the advantages of Godot that make it a great option for mobile game development.

1. Free and Open-Source

One of the biggest advantages of Godot is that it's completely free and open-source. This means that anyone can download, use, and modify the engine without having to pay a dime. This is particularly beneficial for indie developers who may not have the budget for expensive game engines like Unity or Unreal.

2. Lightweight and Fast

Godot is known for being lightweight and fast, which makes it a great choice for mobile game development. It's designed to run smoothly on a wide range of devices, even those with lower-end hardware. This means that games created with Godot are less likely to lag or crash on older phones and tablets.

3. Easy to Use

Godot has a user-friendly interface that makes it easy for developers to create games. It has a drag-and-drop system for creating scenes, nodes, and resources, which can save a lot of time and hassle. Additionally, it has a built-in scripting language called GDScript that's easy to learn and use.

4. Cross-Platform Support

Godot supports a wide range of platforms, including Windows, macOS, Linux, Android, iOS, and HTML5. This makes it easy for developers to create games that can be played on a variety of devices. Additionally, Godot has a built-in export system that allows developers to package their games for distribution on various platforms.

5. Community Support

Finally, Godot has a thriving community of developers who are constantly creating new tools, tutorials, and resources for others to use. This means that if you ever run into a problem or need help with something, there's likely someone in the community who can assist you.

In conclusion, Godot is a great option for mobile game development. Its free and open-source nature, lightweight and fast performance, easy-to-use interface, cross-platform support, and community support all make it a compelling choice for developers looking to create games for mobile devices.

Free and open-source

Free and open-source software has been a game-changer in the world of technology. It has changed the way we think about software development and how we share our work with others. This is especially true in the world of game engines, where free and open-source software has become increasingly popular.

Free and open-source software refers to software that is released under a license that allows users to use, modify, and distribute the software freely. This means that anyone can use the software for any purpose, without having to pay a fee or obtain permission from the original developer.

Additionally, users can modify the software to suit their specific needs, and they can share their modifications with others.

One of the biggest advantages of free and open-source software is that it is often more affordable than proprietary software. This is because there are no licensing fees, which can be a significant expense for developers. Additionally, users can modify the software to suit their specific needs, which can save them time and money in the long run.

Another advantage of free and open-source software is that it is often more customizable than proprietary software. This is because users can modify the software to suit their specific needs, which can give them a competitive advantage in the market. Additionally, users can share their modifications with others, which can lead to a more collaborative and innovative development process.

There are several free and open-source game engines available, including Godot. Godot is a popular game engine that is known for its simplicity, flexibility, and ease of use. It is also free and open-source, which makes it an attractive option for developers who are looking for an affordable and customizable game engine.

In conclusion, free and open-source software has become increasingly popular in the world of game engines. It offers several advantages over proprietary software, including affordability and customization. Godot is a popular free and open-source game engine that is known for its simplicity and flexibility.

Developers who are looking for an affordable and customizable game engine should consider using Godot.

Lightweight and fast

When it comes to developing mobile games, speed and performance are crucial factors that can make or break the success of your game. In order to create a game that runs smoothly on a variety of mobile devices, you need a game engine that is both lightweight and fast. This is where Unity, Unreal, and Godot differ in their approach.

Unity, for example, is known for its fast and efficient performance. The engine is designed to optimize graphics, animations, and other game elements to ensure that the game runs smoothly on mobile devices. Unity also provides support for multiple platforms, including iOS and Android, which allows developers to create games that can be played on a wide range of mobile devices.

On the other hand, Unreal Engine is a more robust game engine with a steep learning curve. However, it is also designed to be fast and efficient, with a focus on high-end graphics and visual effects. Unreal Engine is known for its ability to create highly realistic games with stunning graphics, but this comes at the cost of performance.

Godot is a lightweight game engine that is designed to be fast and efficient while still providing developers with the tools they need to create high-quality games. The engine uses a simplified architecture that makes it easy for developers to create games quickly and efficiently. Godot is also open-source, which means that developers can modify the engine to suit their specific needs.

When it comes to choosing the right mobile game engine, it's important to consider your specific needs and goals. If you're looking for a fast and efficient engine that can support multiple platforms, Unity may be the best choice. If you're looking to create highly realistic games with stunning graphics, Unreal Engine may be the better option.

However, if you're looking for a lightweight engine that is easy to use and modify, Godot may be the best choice.

Ultimately, the choice between Unity, Unreal, and Godot will depend on your specific needs and goals as a mobile game developer. By understanding the strengths and weaknesses of each engine, you can make an informed decision that will help you create the best game possible.

Cross-platform development

Cross-platform development is one of the most important aspects of mobile game development. It refers to the ability of game engines to create games that can run on multiple platforms, such as iOS, Android, Windows, and others. In today's world, where users access games on various devices, cross-platform development is essential for game developers.

Unity, Unreal, and Godot are three of the most popular game engines that offer cross-platform development capabilities. Each engine has its own strengths and weaknesses when it comes to cross-platform development, and choosing the right one for your game can make a big difference in its success.

Unity is known for its excellent cross-platform development capabilities. It supports publishing to over 25 platforms, including mobile, desktop, consoles, and web. Unity's cross-platform development is possible due to its robust scripting language, C#, which allows developers to write code once and run it on multiple platforms.

Unreal, on the other hand, is also a powerful game engine that offers cross-platform development. It supports publishing to iOS, Android, Windows, Mac, Linux, and consoles. Unreal uses C++ as its scripting language, which provides developers with high performance and flexibility in developing games for different platforms.

Godot is a relatively new game engine, but it has gained popularity among indie game developers due to its cross-platform development capabilities. It supports publishing to iOS, Android, Windows, Mac, and Linux. Godot uses its own scripting language, GDScript, which is similar to Python, making it easy for developers to learn and use.

When choosing a game engine for cross-platform development, it's important to consider the specific needs of your game. Each engine has its own strengths and weaknesses, so it's vital to choose the one that best fits your game's requirements.

In conclusion, cross-platform development is a critical aspect of mobile game development. Unity, Unreal, and Godot are three of the most popular game engines that offer cross-platform development capabilities. Each engine has its own strengths and weaknesses, so it's essential to choose the one that is best suited for your game's requirements.

Disadvantages of Godot

Godot is a popular game engine that is known for being lightweight and easy to use. However, like any software, it has its disadvantages that should be taken into consideration before deciding to use it for mobile game development.

One of the biggest disadvantages of Godot is its lack of community support. While it does have a dedicated community, it is much smaller than those of other game engines like Unity and Unreal. This can make it difficult to find answers to specific questions or get help with troubleshooting issues.

Another disadvantage of Godot is its limited resources for learning. While there are some tutorials and documentation available, they are not as extensive as those offered by Unity and Unreal. This means that developers may need to spend more time figuring out how to use the engine and may not have access to as many resources to help them along the way.

Godot also has limited third-party integration options. This can make it difficult to integrate with other tools and services that developers may need to use for mobile game development. Additionally, Godot does not have as many pre-built assets and plugins available compared to other game engines, which can make development more time-consuming.

Finally, Godot may not be the best choice for larger, more complex projects. While it is a great option for smaller indie games, it may struggle with handling larger-scale projects due to its lightweight design. In these cases, Unity and Unreal may be better suited for the job.

In conclusion, while Godot is a great game engine for certain types of mobile game development, it does have its disadvantages. Developers should carefully consider their needs and the scope of their project before deciding whether or not Godot is the right choice for them.

Limited documentation and community support

One of the biggest challenges that developers face when working with game engines is limited documentation and community support. While Unity and Unreal have well-established communities and extensive documentation, Godot lags behind in this aspect.

Unity boasts a vast community of developers who constantly create and share resources, tutorials, and plugins. The official Unity documentation is also comprehensive and easy to navigate. Unreal, on the other hand, has a similarly active community, and Epic Games provides extensive documentation and support to developers.

Godot, however, struggles to compete in this area. The engine's community is relatively small, and the documentation can be difficult to navigate. While there are resources available, they are often outdated or incomplete. This can be frustrating for developers who need quick solutions or are new to the engine.

That being said, Godot's community is growing and improving every day. With more developers adopting the engine, the number of resources and tutorials is increasing. Additionally, the engine's open-source nature means that anyone can contribute to the documentation and create new resources.

For developers who prioritize community support and extensive documentation, Unity and Unreal are the obvious choices. However, for those who value open-source collaboration and a growing community, Godot may be the better option. Ultimately, it comes down to the individual developer's needs and preferences.

Regardless of which engine you choose, it's important to join the community and take advantage of the available resources. Networking with other developers, participating in forums and discussions, and contributing to open-source projects can all help overcome the challenge of limited documentation and community support.

Limited graphics capabilities

Limited graphics capabilities are one of the biggest challenges that game developers face when creating mobile games. While mobile devices have come a long way in terms of processing power and memory, they still have limited graphics capabilities compared to desktop computers and consoles.

This limitation can make it difficult to create visually stunning games on mobile devices.

Unity, Unreal, and Godot are all popular game engines that offer different solutions to this challenge. Unity, for example, provides a range of tools and features that can help developers optimize their games for mobile devices. These tools include the ability to adjust graphics settings, optimize textures, and use different rendering techniques to help reduce the strain on mobile devices.

Unreal, on the other hand, is known for its advanced graphics capabilities. The engine uses a range of advanced rendering techniques, such as dynamic lighting and global illumination, to create visually stunning games. While this may be beneficial for desktop computers and consoles, it can be challenging to optimize these features for mobile devices.

Godot is a lightweight game engine that is designed specifically for mobile devices. The engine uses a range of techniques, such as pre-baked lighting and 2D graphics, to help reduce the strain on mobile devices. While the engine may not offer the same advanced features as Unity or Unreal, it provides a solid foundation for developers to create visually appealing games on mobile devices.

In conclusion, limited graphics capabilities are a challenge that all mobile game developers face. However, by choosing the right game engine, developers can overcome this challenge and create visually stunning games on mobile devices.

Unity, Unreal, and Godot are all popular game engines that offer different solutions to this challenge, and developers should choose the engine that best suits their needs and goals.

Smaller user base

One of the key considerations when choosing a game engine for mobile development is the size of its user base. This is because a larger user base means more support, more resources, and more opportunities for collaboration.

Unity and Unreal have been around for a long time and have built up sizable communities of developers and users. This means that there are a lot of resources available online, such as tutorials, forums, and plugins, that can help you with your game development projects.

In addition, the larger user base means that there are more opportunities for collaboration and networking, which can be valuable for building your skills and expanding your career.

Godot, on the other hand, is a newer game engine and has a smaller user base. This means that there are fewer resources available online and fewer opportunities for collaboration. However, the Godot community is growing rapidly, and there are still plenty of resources available, such as the official documentation, community forums, and user-created tutorials and plugins.

One advantage of a smaller user base is that there is less competition for attention and resources. In the case of Godot, this means that the developers have been able to focus on creating a game engine that is tailored to the needs of indie developers and hobbyists, rather than trying to appeal to a broad range of users.

This has resulted in a game engine that is lightweight, easy to use, and highly customizable, making it ideal for small-scale development projects.

Ultimately, the size of the user base should not be the only factor you consider when choosing a game engine for mobile development. It is important to evaluate each engine based on its features, performance, ease of use, and other factors that are important to you.

However, the size of the user base can be a useful indicator of the level of support and resources you can expect to find when working with a particular engine.

Case studies

Case studies are a great way to understand how different game engines perform in real-world scenarios. In this subchapter, we will take a closer look at some of the popular mobile games developed using Unity, Unreal, and Godot.

Let's start with Unity, which is one of the most widely used game engines in the mobile gaming industry. One of the most successful mobile games developed using Unity is "Temple Run." This endless runner game has been downloaded over a billion times and is still popular among mobile gamers. Another notable game developed using Unity is "Pokémon Go.

" This game uses augmented reality technology and became a global phenomenon when it was released in 2016.

Moving on to Unreal, which is known for its high-quality graphics and rendering capabilities. "Infinity Blade" is a mobile game developed using Unreal, and it was one of the first mobile games to showcase the true potential of the engine. The game features stunning visuals, intuitive controls, and an engaging storyline. Another popular game developed using Unreal is "Real Racing 3.

" This game has been praised for its realistic graphics and physics-based gameplay.

Finally, let's take a look at Godot, a free and open-source game engine that has been gaining popularity among indie game developers. "Hyper Light Drifter" is a game developed using Godot, and it has received critical acclaim for its stunning visuals and challenging gameplay. Another notable game developed using Godot is "Papers, Please.

" This game puts players in the shoes of an immigration officer and challenges them to make difficult decisions.

In conclusion, these case studies demonstrate the capabilities of Unity, Unreal, and Godot in developing successful mobile games. Each game engine has its strengths and weaknesses, and it's up to developers to choose the one that best suits their needs. By studying these case studies, developers can gain valuable insights into the mobile game development process and make informed decisions.

Dead Cells

Dead Cells is a popular indie game that was developed by Motion Twin and released in 2018. It is a unique mix of roguelike and metroidvania genres, with procedurally generated levels and a wide variety of weapons and abilities to unlock. The game has been praised for its tight gameplay, challenging difficulty, and beautiful pixel art graphics.

Dead Cells was developed using the Unity game engine, which is one of the most popular game engines used in the mobile gaming industry. Unity is known for its ease of use, versatility, and powerful features, which make it a great choice for developing games of all genres and sizes.

One of the key strengths of Unity is its ability to handle complex 2D and 3D graphics, which is essential for games like Dead Cells that rely heavily on visual design. The engine also comes with a range of tools and plugins that make it easy to create animations, particle effects, and other visual elements that add to the game's overall atmosphere.

In addition to its graphics capabilities, Unity is also a great choice for mobile game development because of its cross-platform support. This means that developers can create a game for one platform, such as iOS or Android, and easily port it to other platforms without having to rewrite the entire game from scratch.

Another advantage of using Unity for mobile game development is its active community of developers and users, who provide support, tutorials, and resources for other developers. This makes it easy to get started with Unity and to learn how to use its features effectively.

Overall, Dead Cells is a great example of what can be achieved with the Unity game engine. Its success demonstrates that Unity is a powerful and versatile tool that can be used to create high-quality mobile games of all genres and sizes. Whether you're a hobbyist developer or a professional game studio, Unity is definitely worth considering as your game engine of choice.

Hollow Knight

Hollow Knight is a critically acclaimed action-adventure game developed and published by Team Cherry. The game was released in 2017 and has since gained a massive following due to its stunning visuals, engaging gameplay, and immersive storyline.

Hollow Knight is built using the Unity game engine, which is known for its flexibility, scalability, and ease of use. The game engine has been around for over a decade and has been used to develop some of the most popular games on the market, including Angry Birds, Temple Run, and Monument Valley.

One of the key features of the Unity game engine that makes it an excellent choice for developing games like Hollow Knight is its ability to handle 2D graphics with ease. The game's stunning visuals are a testament to the engine's capabilities, and it showcases how Unity can help developers create games that are both visually stunning and engaging.

Furthermore, Unity's robust scripting language, C#, makes it easy for developers to create complex gameplay mechanics and AI systems. This is evident in Hollow Knight's intricate combat system, which requires precise timing and strategy to master.

Another reason why Unity is an excellent choice for developing games like Hollow Knight is its cross-platform compatibility. The game is available on multiple platforms, including Windows, macOS, Linux, Nintendo Switch, PlayStation 4, and Xbox One. Unity makes it easy for developers to port their game to multiple platforms without having to rewrite the entire codebase.

In conclusion, Hollow Knight is an excellent example of how Unity can be used to create visually stunning and engaging games. The game's success is a testament to the engine's capabilities, and it showcases how Unity can help developers create games that are both fun and challenging. If you're looking to develop a game like Hollow Knight, Unity is definitely worth considering.

Night in the Woods

Night in the Woods is one of the most popular games to have been developed using the Unity game engine. This game is an adventure game that takes you on a journey through the eyes of a cat named Mae, who has returned to her hometown after dropping out of college. The game is set in a small town called Possum Springs, which is full of strange and mysterious events.

The game's visuals are stunning, with a hand-drawn art style that gives the game a unique and charming look. The game's graphics are also enhanced by Unity's lighting system, which creates a sense of depth and realism that makes the game feel more immersive.

One of the key features of Night in the Woods is the game's branching narrative. The game is full of choices that you can make that will alter the course of the story. This feature is made possible by Unity's powerful scripting system, which allows developers to create complex dialog trees and decision-making systems.

The game also features a unique soundtrack that perfectly captures the game's tone and atmosphere. The music is composed by Alec Holowka, who sadly passed away in 2019. The soundtrack is a testament to his talent as a composer, and it adds an extra layer of emotion to an already emotionally charged game.

Overall, Night in the Woods is a perfect example of what can be achieved with the Unity game engine. The game's visuals, narrative, and music all come together to create a truly unforgettable experience. If you're interested in developing adventure games or games with branching narratives, then Unity is definitely a game engine that you should consider.

Comparison

Comparison chart

A comparison chart is a useful tool for anyone looking to choose between Unity, Unreal, and Godot as their mobile game engine. This chart provides a side-by-side comparison of the key features and capabilities of each engine, allowing you to make an informed decision about which one is right for you.

At a high level, all three engines offer similar functionality, including 3D graphics, physics simulation, and support for multiple platforms. However, there are some key differences between the three that may influence your decision.

Unity is a popular choice for mobile game development due to its ease of use and extensive documentation. It offers a large number of pre-built assets and tools, making it easy for beginners to get started quickly. It also has robust support for 2D graphics and is known for its excellent performance on mobile devices.

Unreal, on the other hand, is a more powerful engine that is better suited to larger, more complex games. It offers advanced features such as high-quality lighting and shading, advanced physics simulation, and support for virtual reality. However, it has a steeper learning curve and requires more technical expertise to use effectively.

Godot is a newer engine that has gained popularity in recent years due to its open-source nature and ease of use. It offers a flexible scripting language and an intuitive interface, making it a good choice for smaller indie games. However, it currently lacks some of the advanced features of Unity and Unreal, and may not be the best choice for larger, more complex projects.

Ultimately, the choice between Unity, Unreal, and Godot will depend on your specific needs and goals as a developer. A comparison chart can help you to evaluate the strengths and weaknesses of each engine and make an informed decision about which one to use for your mobile game development project.

Factors to consider when choosing a game engine

Choosing the right game engine is a crucial decision for any game developer. With so many options available, it can be overwhelming to determine which one is best suited for your project. In this subchapter, we'll discuss the factors you should consider when choosing a game engine for your mobile game.

1. Platform Compatibility: One of the most important factors to consider when choosing a game engine is platform compatibility. Your game engine should support the platform(s) you plan to release your game on. Unity and Unreal both support a wide range of platforms, including iOS, Android, and Windows, while Godot only supports iOS and Android.

2. Ease of Use: Another important factor to consider is how easy the game engine is to use. Unity and Unreal have a steeper learning curve, while Godot is more beginner-friendly. If you're new to game development, Godot might be the better option.

3. Graphics and Performance: Graphics and performance are essential for any game. Unreal Engine is known for its impressive graphics capabilities, while Unity is more versatile in terms of graphics and performance. Godot is less powerful than the other two engines, but it's still capable of producing visually appealing games.

4. Pricing and Licensing: The cost of the game engine is also a crucial consideration. Unity and Unreal both offer free versions, but you'll need to pay for certain features. Godot, on the other hand, is completely free and open-source.

5. Community and Support: Having a strong community and support system can be extremely helpful when working with a game engine. Unity and Unreal have large and active communities, while Godot's community is smaller but growing.

Ultimately, the game engine you choose depends on your specific needs and preferences. Unity is a great all-around choice, while Unreal is ideal for projects that require high-end graphics. Godot is an excellent option for indie developers on a budget. Whatever you choose, make sure the game engine you select aligns with your goals and capabilities.

Budget

Budget

One of the most important factors to consider when choosing a mobile game engine is the budget. Different engines have different pricing models, and it's important to understand what you'll be paying for and how much it will cost.

Unity offers a variety of pricing plans, starting with a free Personal plan that includes basic features and can be used to create games with revenue of up to $100,000 per year. The Plus plan costs $35 per month and includes additional features such as analytics and cloud storage, while the Pro plan costs $125 per month and includes even more features such as performance reporting and custom splash screens.

Unity also offers a custom Enterprise plan for larger studios that need more support and customization.

Unreal Engine, on the other hand, is free to use, but charges a 5% royalty on gross revenue after the first $3,000 per product, per quarter. This means that if you make $10,000 in a quarter from a game made with Unreal Engine, you'll owe $350 in royalties. Unreal Engine also offers a custom licensing option for larger studios that need more control over their development process.

Godot is completely free and open-source, with no licensing fees or royalties. However, the engine relies heavily on community contributions and may not have the same level of support and resources as Unity or Unreal Engine.

When considering budget, it's important to also think about the cost of additional assets and plugins that may be necessary for your game. Unity and Unreal Engine have large marketplaces with a variety of assets and plugins available for purchase, while Godot's marketplace is still growing.

Ultimately, the budget will play a significant role in determining which mobile game engine is right for you. If you're just starting out and have a limited budget, Godot may be the best option. If you have more resources and need more features, Unity or Unreal Engine may be a better choice.

It's important to carefully evaluate the pricing plans and additional costs of each engine to make an informed decision.

Development goals

Development Goals

When it comes to choosing a game engine for mobile game development, it's important to have a clear set of development goals in mind. Each engine has its own strengths and weaknesses, and understanding what you want to achieve will help you make an informed decision.

One of the most important development goals is performance. Mobile devices have limited processing power, and games that don't run smoothly can quickly turn players off. Unity, Unreal, and Godot all have their own approaches to optimizing performance, but each engine has its own limitations as well.

Another important development goal is ease of use. Game development can be a complex process, and working with an engine that is easy to understand and use can save a lot of time and frustration. Godot, for example, is known for its user-friendly interface and intuitive scripting language, while Unreal can be more challenging for beginners.

Compatibility with different platforms is also an important consideration. Unity and Unreal both offer robust support for multiple platforms, including iOS and Android, while Godot is still working on expanding its support for mobile devices.

When it comes to graphics, Unreal is often considered the industry standard. Its advanced rendering capabilities allow for stunning visuals, but this comes at the cost of performance on mobile devices. Unity, on the other hand, provides a balance between performance and graphics quality, while Godot offers a simpler, more lightweight approach to graphics.

Ultimately, the development goals that matter most to you will depend on the type of game you're developing and your personal preferences as a developer. Understanding the strengths and weaknesses of each engine can help you make an informed decision and choose the engine that is right for you.

Team size and experience

Team size and experience are two critical factors to consider when choosing a mobile game engine. The size of your team will determine the complexity of the game you can create, while the experience of your team members will affect how efficiently you can work with the engine.

Unity is a great choice for small to medium-sized teams, as it has a vast community of developers and a wealth of resources available online. Unity's visual scripting tool, Bolt, also makes it easy for non-programmers to create complex game logic.

However, Unity's learning curve can be steep for beginners, and its codebase can become cluttered and difficult to manage for larger teams.

Unreal is an excellent choice for larger teams with experienced developers, as its codebase is well-organized and its C++ programming language offers greater control over performance and memory management. Unreal's Blueprint visual scripting system is also powerful but easier to learn than Unity's Bolt.

However, Unreal's complexity can be overwhelming for beginners, and its community is smaller than Unity's.

Godot is a great choice for small teams with limited experience or for solo developers, as it has a user-friendly interface and a simple scripting language. Godot's built-in node-based editor also makes it easy to create complex game logic without the need for coding. However, Godot's community is still growing, and its resources are not as abundant as Unity or Unreal.

Ultimately, the size and experience of your team will determine which mobile game engine is right for you. If you have a small team with limited experience, Godot may be the best choice for you. If you have a larger team with experienced developers, Unreal may be the way to go. And if you have a medium-sized team with varying levels of experience, Unity may be the most versatile option.

Whichever engine you choose, make sure to consider your team's strengths and weaknesses and choose the engine that best fits your needs. With the right tools and a talented team, you can create a successful mobile game that stands out in a competitive market.

Unity vs. Unreal vs. Godot

Unity, Unreal, and Godot are three of the most popular game engines in the market today. Each of these engines comes with its own set of features, advantages, and disadvantages. As a mobile game developer, choosing the right game engine can be a challenging task. This subchapter will compare Unity, Unreal, and Godot to help you make an informed decision.

Unity is a widely used game engine that is suitable for both 2D and 3D games. It offers a wide range of tools and features that make game development easier and faster. Unity is easy to learn, and there is a large community of developers who provide support and resources.

However, Unity has a steep learning curve when it comes to advanced features like shader programming, and it can be expensive for commercial use.

Unreal, on the other hand, is a powerful game engine that is specifically designed for 3D games. It is widely used in the gaming industry and offers advanced features like real-time lighting and physics simulation. Unreal is also free to use, and there is a large community of developers who provide support and resources.

However, Unreal has a steep learning curve, and it requires a high-end computer to run smoothly.

Godot is a lightweight game engine that is suitable for both 2D and 3D games. It is free to use, and it offers a wide range of tools and features that make game development easier and faster. Godot has a small learning curve, and it is easy to use for beginners. However, Godot is not as powerful as Unity or Unreal, and it lacks some of the advanced features that these engines offer.

In conclusion, choosing the right game engine depends on your specific needs and requirements. If you are looking for a game engine that is easy to learn and use, Unity or Godot might be the right choice for you. If you are looking for a game engine that offers advanced features and is widely used in the gaming industry, Unreal might be the right choice for you.

It is important to consider your budget, skill level, and project requirements before making a decision.

Graphics capabilities

Graphics capabilities are an essential aspect of any mobile game engine. Unity, Unreal, and Godot all have their unique strengths and weaknesses in this area. A comparison of each engine's graphics capabilities can help you decide which one is right for your mobile game development needs.

Unity is known for its ease of use in creating 2D and 3D graphics. The engine provides a variety of tools and resources to help developers create stunning and engaging graphics for their games. Unity's graphics pipeline is optimized for mobile devices, which means that the engine is capable of rendering high-quality graphics while maintaining a smooth frame rate.

Additionally, Unity has a vast library of pre-built assets, which can save developers time and effort in creating graphics from scratch.

Unreal, on the other hand, is known for its advanced graphics capabilities. The engine uses proprietary rendering technology that enables developers to create incredibly detailed and realistic graphics. Unreal's graphics pipeline is optimized for high-end devices, which means that the engine can push the limits of mobile hardware.

Unreal also has a vast library of pre-built assets, which can help developers create stunning graphics quickly.

Godot's graphics capabilities are somewhat more limited than Unity and Unreal. However, the engine provides a variety of tools and resources to help developers create simple yet engaging graphics for their games. Godot's graphics pipeline is optimized for low-end devices, which means that the engine can run on a wide range of devices.

Additionally, Godot has a vast library of pre-built assets, which can help developers create graphics quickly.

In conclusion, Unity, Unreal, and Godot all have their unique strengths and weaknesses in graphics capabilities. Unity is easy to use and optimized for mobile devices, while Unreal is advanced and optimized for high-end devices. Godot is simple and optimized for low-end devices.

The choice of game engine will depend on the type of game you want to create and the level of graphics detail required.

Ease of use

Ease of use is one of the most important factors to consider when choosing a mobile game engine. As an aspiring game developer, you want to focus on creating amazing games, not wrestling with complicated tools and convoluted workflows. Unity, Unreal, and Godot all have their unique strengths and weaknesses when it comes to ease of use, so let's take a closer look at each one.

Unity is widely regarded as one of the most user-friendly game engines out there. Its drag-and-drop interface, visual scripting system, and comprehensive documentation make it easy for beginners to jump in and start creating games in no time. Unity's asset store also provides a wealth of ready-made assets and plugins that can save you hours of work.

Unreal, on the other hand, has a steeper learning curve, but it's not without its advantages. Its Blueprint visual scripting system is powerful and flexible, allowing you to create complex game logic without writing a single line of code. Unreal's visual editor is also incredibly robust, giving you complete control over every aspect of your game's design and functionality.

Godot is a relative newcomer to the game engine scene, but it's quickly gaining popularity thanks to its ease of use and open-source nature. Its intuitive interface and simple scripting language make it a great option for beginners, while its node-based visual scripting system offers more advanced users a lot of flexibility and power.

Ultimately, the ease of use of a game engine will depend on your personal skill level, preferences, and goals. If you're just starting out and want to get up and running quickly, Unity may be the best choice for you. If you're willing to put in the time to learn a more complex tool, Unreal may offer the most flexibility and control.

And if you're looking for a free and open-source option that's both user-friendly and powerful, Godot is definitely worth checking out.

In conclusion, choosing the right mobile game engine for your needs requires careful consideration of a variety of factors, including ease of use. By taking the time to evaluate the strengths and weaknesses of Unity, Unreal, and Godot, you'll be well on your way to making an informed decision that will help you achieve your game development goals.

Community support

Community support is a crucial factor to consider when choosing a mobile game engine. It refers to the network of developers, programmers, and enthusiasts who use the engine and contribute to its development by sharing knowledge, creating plugins, and offering support forums.

A strong community can make all the difference in your game development journey, so let's take a closer look at how Unity, Unreal, and Godot stack up in this regard.

Unity has one of the largest and most active communities in the game development world. With over 2 million registered users, the Unity community offers a wealth of resources, including forums, tutorials, and a vast library of plugins and assets. Unity also hosts an annual conference, Unite, where developers from all over the world gather to share their knowledge and showcase their games.

The Unity Asset Store is also a great resource, where developers can buy and sell assets, plugins, and tools. Overall, Unity's community is vibrant and supportive, making it a great choice for developers looking for a strong network of peers.

Unreal Engine also has a strong community, with over a million registered users. The Unreal Engine forums are a great place to get help and advice, and the engine's documentation is extensive and well-organized. Unreal also hosts an annual conference, Unreal Fest, where developers can network and learn from experts.

The Unreal Marketplace offers a range of assets and plugins, although it's not as extensive as Unity's Asset Store. Overall, Unreal's community is active and helpful, but it may not be as extensive as Unity's.

Godot's community is smaller than Unity and Unreal's, but it's growing rapidly. The engine's official forums are a great resource for getting help and advice, and the community is known for being welcoming and supportive. Godot doesn't have a centralized asset store like Unity and Unreal, but there are many third-party sites that offer free and paid assets and plugins.

Overall, Godot's community may not be as large as Unity and Unreal's, but it's still a great choice for developers looking for a supportive network of peers.

In conclusion, community support is an important factor to consider when choosing a mobile game engine. Unity and Unreal have large and active communities, while Godot's community is smaller but growing. All three engines offer a wealth of resources and support, making them great choices for developers looking to join a vibrant and supportive community.

Cross-platform development

Cross-platform development is one of the most important aspects of game development today. With the rise of mobile gaming, developers need to create games that can be played on a range of devices, from smartphones to tablets to PCs. This is where cross-platform development comes in.

Cross-platform development is the process of developing games that can run on multiple platforms, including Windows, macOS, Linux, iOS, and Android. It allows developers to create games that can reach a wider audience, and it can reduce development costs and time.

Unity, Unreal, and Godot are three of the most popular mobile game engines available today, and each offers its own unique set of features and tools for cross-platform development.

Unity is known for its ease of use and flexibility. It offers a range of features and tools for developing cross-platform games, including support for multiple platforms, a visual editor, and a scripting language called C#. Unity also offers a range of plugins and extensions that can help developers create games faster and more efficiently.

Unreal is known for its high-quality graphics and advanced physics engine. It offers a range of features and tools for developing cross-platform games, including support for multiple platforms, a visual editor, and a scripting language called Blueprint. Unreal also offers a range of plugins and extensions that can help developers create games with stunning visuals and realistic physics.

Godot is known for its lightweight design and ease of use. It offers a range of features and tools for developing cross-platform games, including support for multiple platforms, a visual editor, and a scripting language called GDScript. Godot also offers a range of plugins and extensions that can help developers create games quickly and efficiently.

In conclusion, cross-platform development is an essential aspect of mobile game development, and Unity, Unreal, and Godot are three of the most popular mobile game engines available today. Each offers its own unique set of features and tools for cross-platform development, and choosing the right engine depends on your specific needs and goals as a developer.

Conclusion

In conclusion, choosing the right mobile game engine for your project can be a daunting task. Unity, Unreal, and Godot all have their unique strengths and weaknesses, and each one is suited for different types of games and developers.

If you're looking for a user-friendly engine with a low learning curve, Godot might be the best option for you. It's open-source, free, and it has a visual scripting system that allows you to create games without writing a single line of code.

On the other hand, if you need a powerful engine with advanced features and a large community of developers and resources, Unity might be the way to go. It has a massive marketplace with a vast selection of assets, plugins, and tools, and it's widely used across the industry.

If you're looking to create high-quality, visually stunning games with cutting-edge graphics and effects, then Unreal might be the best option for you. It's the most powerful engine of the three, and it's widely used in the AAA game industry.

Ultimately, the choice of mobile game engine will depend on your specific needs and goals as a developer. Whether you're a beginner or an experienced game developer, each engine has its own set of features and benefits that can help you bring your vision to life.

We hope this book has provided you with valuable insights into the differences between Unity, Unreal, and Godot, and helped you make an informed decision about which engine is right for you. Remember, no matter which engine you choose, the most important thing is to have fun and enjoy the process of creating your game!

Conclusion

Recap of the book

After exploring the different aspects of Unity, Unreal, and Godot, it's time to recap the key takeaways from this book.

First and foremost, it's important to understand that Unity, Unreal, and Godot are all powerful game engines that offer unique features and capabilities. The choice between these engines largely depends on your specific needs and preferences as a game developer.

When it comes to ease of use and accessibility, Unity is often considered the best option. Its user-friendly interface and extensive documentation make it easy for beginners to get started with game development. On the other hand, Unreal is known for its advanced graphics capabilities and flexibility in terms of customization.

It's a great option for developers who want full control over their game's visuals and mechanics.

Godot, meanwhile, is a relatively new player in the game engine space but has quickly gained a following among indie game developers. It's known for its lightweight design and open-source nature, making it an attractive option for those on a tight budget.

In terms of performance, all three engines are capable of creating high-quality mobile games. However, Unreal's graphics capabilities give it a slight edge over Unity and Godot when it comes to creating visually stunning games.

When it comes to pricing, Unity and Godot both offer free options, while Unreal requires a 5% royalty fee on gross revenue. However, it's important to note that all three engines offer paid options with additional features and support.

Ultimately, the choice between Unity, Unreal, and Godot comes down to your specific needs and preferences as a game developer. Whether you prioritize ease of use, advanced graphics capabilities, or budget-friendliness, there's an engine out there that will be the perfect fit for you.

In summary, this book has provided an in-depth comparison of Unity, Unreal, and Godot, highlighting their unique features, benefits, and drawbacks. By understanding the differences between these engines, you can make an informed decision about which one will best suit your game development needs.

Final thoughts

In conclusion, choosing the right mobile game engine is a crucial decision for any game developer. Unity, Unreal, and Godot are three of the most popular game engines in the market, and each one has its own set of advantages and disadvantages.

Unity is an excellent choice for beginners or small teams as it is easy to learn and offers a wide range of features. It also has a massive community of developers who share their knowledge and support each other. However, Unity can be expensive for larger teams, and its 2D capabilities are not as strong as its 3D capabilities.

Unreal, on the other hand, is a powerful game engine that offers incredible graphics and realistic gameplay. It is ideal for developing high-end games and has a robust toolset for creating complex game mechanics. However, it has a steep learning curve and requires a high-end computer to run smoothly.

Godot is a free and open-source game engine that offers a lightweight and easy-to-use platform. It is ideal for 2D games and has a simple scripting language that makes it easy for beginners to learn. However, it lacks the advanced features of Unity and Unreal, and its community of developers is relatively small.

Ultimately, choosing the right mobile game engine depends on your specific needs and preferences. You should consider factors such as your budget, team size, and game genre before making a decision.

It is also essential to keep in mind that game development is a constantly evolving field, and new technologies and tools may emerge in the future that could change the game engine landscape.

In summary, Unity, Unreal, and Godot are all excellent game engines, and each one has its own strengths and weaknesses. By understanding these differences and considering your specific needs, you can choose the right engine that will help you create the best mobile game possible.

Resources and further reading

Resources and Further Reading

If you're interested in learning more about mobile game engines and their capabilities, there are plenty of resources available to you. Here are a few suggestions for further reading:

1. Unity's official documentation: Unity offers a comprehensive set of documentation for developers, covering everything from getting started to more advanced topics like physics and AI. Their website also includes tutorials and sample projects that can help you get started.

2. Unreal's official documentation: Unreal also offers extensive documentation for developers, along with a variety of tutorials and sample projects. Their website also includes a community forum where developers can ask questions and share knowledge.

3. Godot's official documentation: Godot's documentation is also quite thorough, and their website includes tutorials and sample projects as well. In addition, Godot offers a community forum where developers can connect and share ideas.

4. "Learning C# by Developing Games with Unity" by Harrison Ferrone: This book is a great resource for those who are new to C# programming and want to learn how to develop games using Unity. It covers topics like game mechanics, graphics, and audio, and includes plenty of hands-on exercises to help you practice your skills.

5. "Unreal Engine 4 Game Development in 24 Hours" by Aram Cookson: This book is geared toward beginners who want to learn the basics of game development using Unreal Engine 4. It covers topics like creating game logic, designing levels, and optimizing performance.

6. "Godot Engine Game Development Projects" by Chris Bradfield: This book offers a series of projects that teach you how to develop games using Godot. It covers topics like 2D platformers, puzzle games, and multiplayer games, and includes plenty of code samples and explanations.

Whether you're just starting out or you're an experienced developer looking to expand your skills, these resources can help you learn more about the capabilities of Unity, Unreal, and Godot. With the right tools and knowledge, you can create amazing mobile games that engage and entertain players around the world.

Acknowledgments

Acknowledgments

Writing a book is never a one-man show. It takes a team of dedicated individuals to make it happen. I would like to express my deepest gratitude to everyone who helped me bring this project to fruition.

First and foremost, I would like to thank my family for their unwavering support and encouragement throughout this journey. Their love and understanding have been my constant source of motivation.

I would also like to extend my heartfelt thanks to my editor, who provided invaluable guidance and feedback that helped me shape this book into its final form. Their keen eye for detail and commitment to excellence have been instrumental in making this book the best it can be.

I am also deeply grateful to the developers behind Unity, Unreal, and Godot, for creating such powerful and versatile game engines that have revolutionized the mobile gaming industry. Their dedication to innovation and excellence has inspired countless developers around the world, and I am honored to have been able to showcase their work in this book.

Last but not least, I would like to thank the readers of this book. Your interest and support mean the world to me, and I hope that this book will provide you with valuable insights and guidance as you navigate the world of mobile game development.

In conclusion, I am humbled and grateful to everyone who has contributed to this project in one way or another. Without your help, this book would not have been possible. Thank you all from the bottom of my heart.